This book belongs to

....

MY FAMOUS MASTERPIECE

1

Print out one of the famous works of art we discussed in class.

Paste it in the box here.

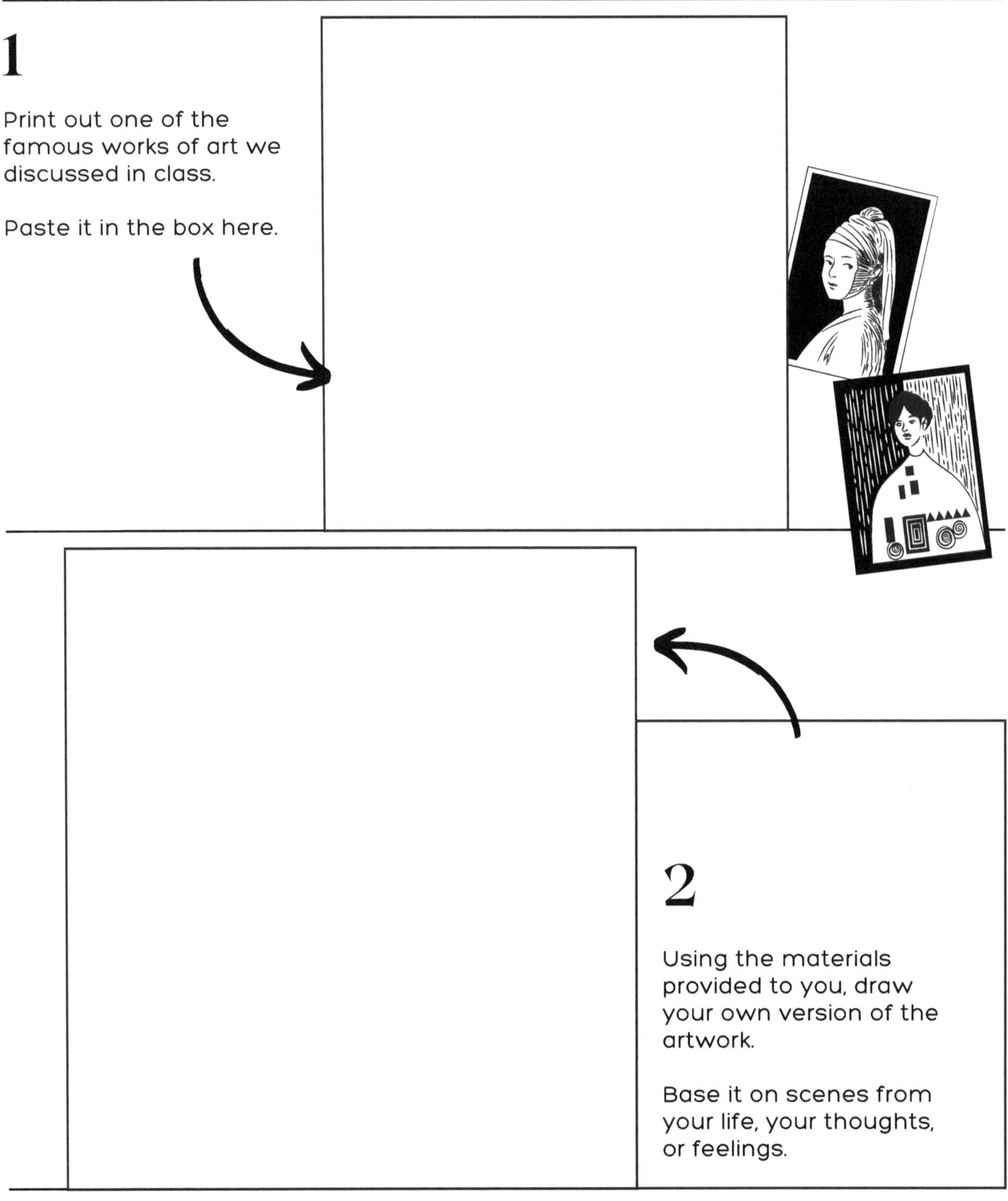

2

Using the materials provided to you, draw your own version of the artwork.

Base it on scenes from your life, your thoughts, or feelings.

MATH DICE GAME

Learn how to add using dice!

Directions: Throw two dice and add the numbers that are on top of the two dice when they land. Write that number down. Now your partner must do the same. Do this ten times, so each person throws the dice ten times. Add up the ten numbers that you have written down. The winner is the one with the highest number.

Essay Writing Exercise

Write an essay based on this prompt:

Think back to a time when you accidentally broke something at home. How did you feel? What happened? Share your thoughts and emotions at the time and what happened afterwards.

A MIX OF MEDIUMS

In the boxes below, use the materials indicated to create your own artwork.

Each artwork should answer the question:

If I could create my own planet, what would it look like?

WATERCOLOR

COLOR PENCILS

OIL PASTEL

GRAPHITE

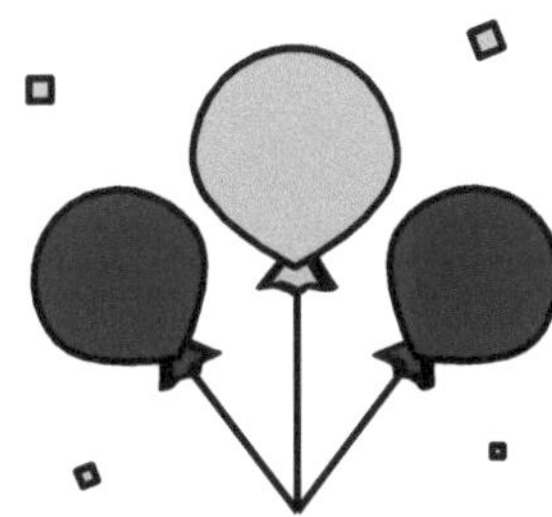

Greater Than, Less Than

Color in the object that shows the number that is less.

Color in the object that shows the number that is greater.

Color in the numbers that are greater than 2 but less than 8.

Draw a comic strip about your favorite pet

Comic Title:

Patterns.

Color in the patterns as instructed.

Color in an AB pattern.

Color in an ABC pattern.

Color in an ABB pattern.

Color in your own pattern.

Great or Less Than Worksheet

Circle the > or < symbol. Remember the symbol points to the number that is less.

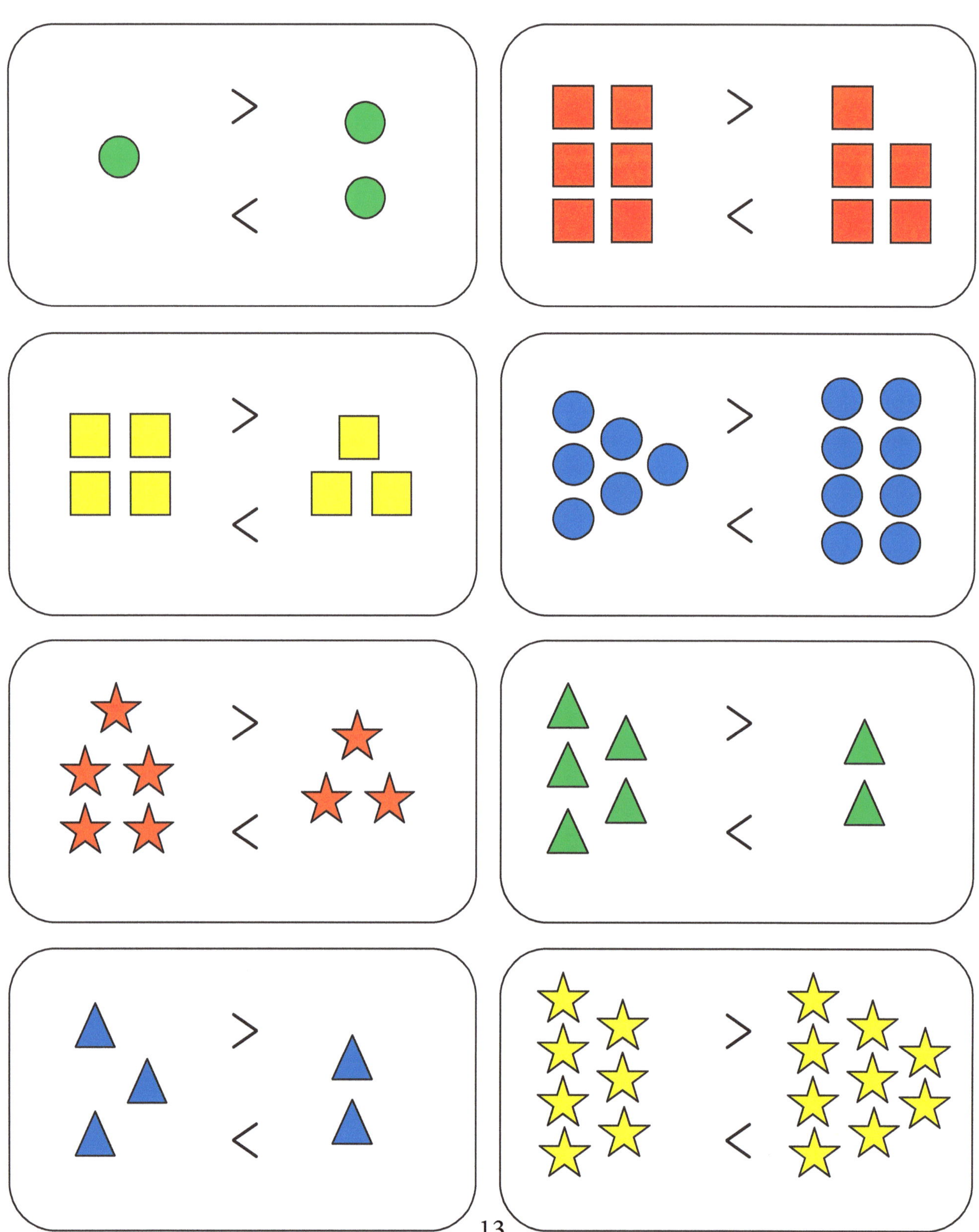

Let's draw a picture!

Draw your favorite food

The Colorful Butterfly

Solve the sums in the boxes to work out what
colours they should be!

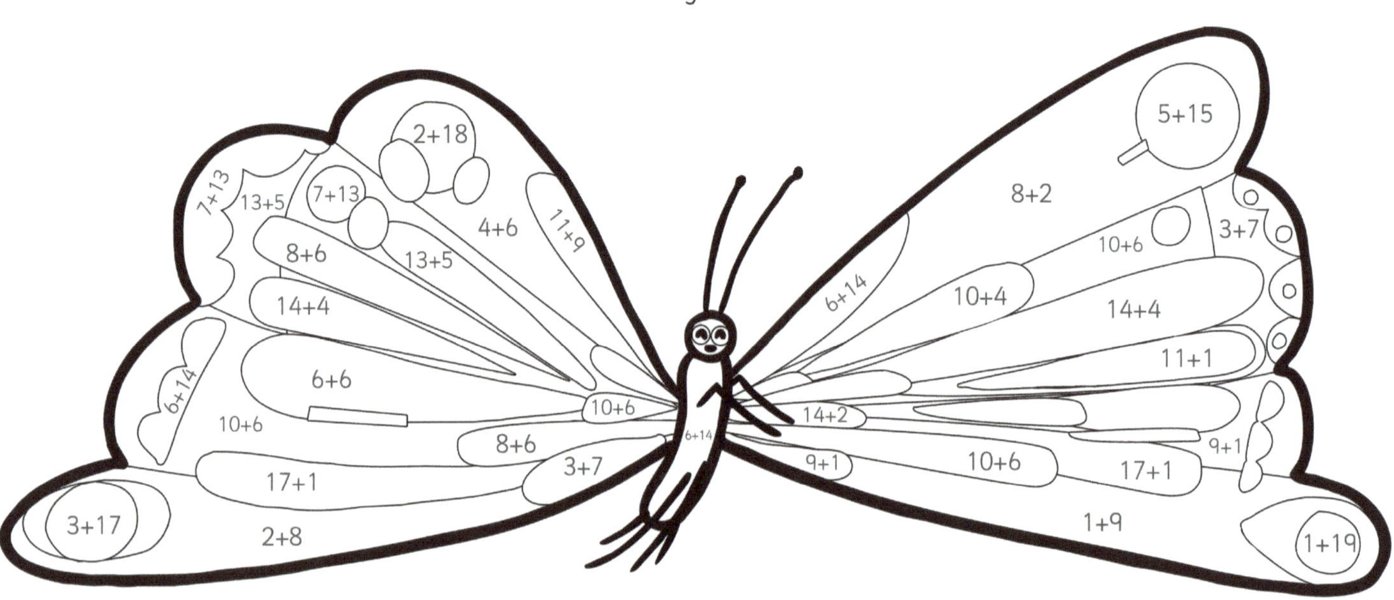

| 10 = Red | 12 = Blue | 14 = Orange |
| 16 = Pink | 18 = Purple | 20 = Yellow |

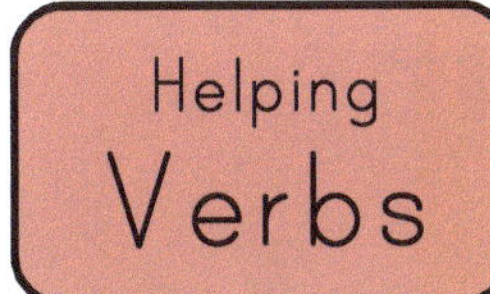

Grammar Worksheet
Helping Verbs

Read the sentences below. Circle the helping verbs and underline the action verb.

1. I can jump rope for two minutes without stopping!

2. I may ask for help if this homework is too hard.

3. Kelly had tried her best on the test.

4. My friends and I are watching a movie on television.

5. Dad could help the plumber fix the pipe.

6. Steven has forgotten his homework often this year.

7. My cousins were planning a trip to Disney World.

8. We will play soccer on Saturday morning.

9. Megan and Becky have gone to the library already.

10. I am going to pick flowers for my Mom.

11. My brother might be late for dinner.

12. My bike is making a strange noise.

Now it is your turn to write a sentence of your own on the lines below. It should have a helping verb and an action verb. After you write the sentence, circle the helping verb and underline the action verb.

____

- -

____

Let's practice our handwriting...

As neatly as you can, write about your favorite hobby.

Match the Action Verbs

Match the verbs in the work bank with the right picture.

| rip   trip   sit   cry   run   sleep |

katelyn's flowers

Put these pictures in the right order to make a story.
Write 1, 2, 3 or 4 in the boxes.

Let's draw a picture!

Draw your house

DOT-TO-DOT

Join the dots to meet our frosty friend!
Then color him in!

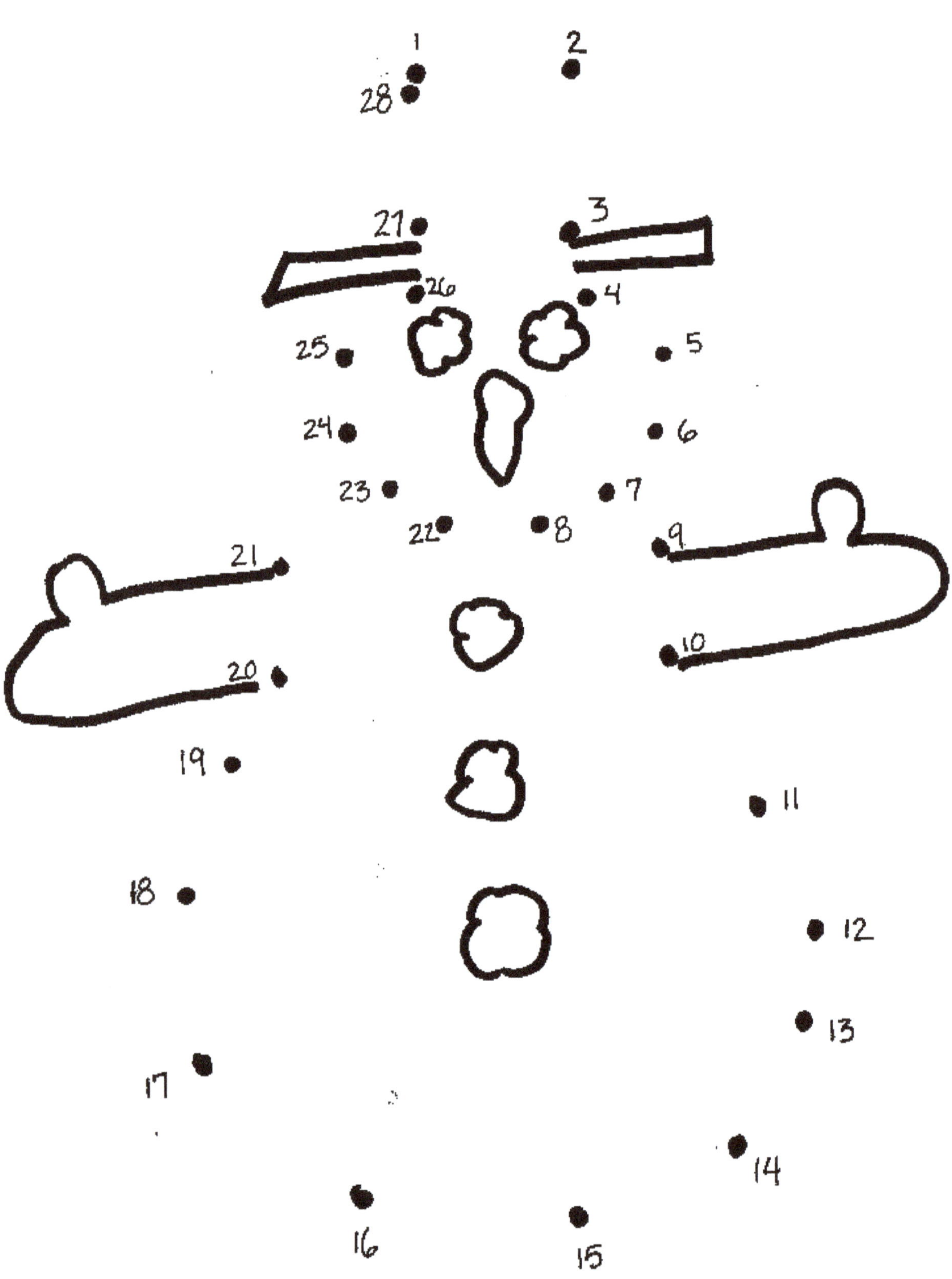

PAYING UP

LET'S PRACTICE ROUNDING UP!

Paul needs to prepare his payment at the supermarket. Round up the prices of the following items, so Paul can pay and get his change:

ITEMS	STORE PRICE	ROUNDED PRICE
1 BOX OF TOOTHPASTE	**$2.10**	
1 BAG OF APPLES	**$5.15**	
1 BAG OF CHIPS	**$3.50**	
1 BOTTLE OF ORANGE JUICE	**$5.35**	

FISHING FOR ANSWERS

A FUN GAME ABOUT NUMBERS

Name _________________ Section _________________

Date _________________ Score _________________

Directions: Solve the equation and fill in the answer.

1.) $5 + \_\_ = 10$

2.) $26 - 14 = \_\_$

3.) $\_\_ + \_\_ = 47$

4.) $\_\_ - 6 = 32$

5.) $15 + \_\_ = 50$

6.) $\_\_ + \_\_ = 26$

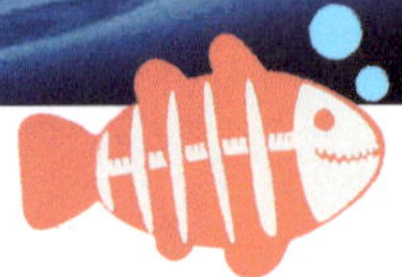

CREATE A FARM

MR. SHEPHERD'S DREAM

Mr. Shepherd has a dream of building his own farm. The first step to realizing this is to figure out the exact area to plot his land. The next is to find the perimeter to build his fence. Help him find these numbers quick!

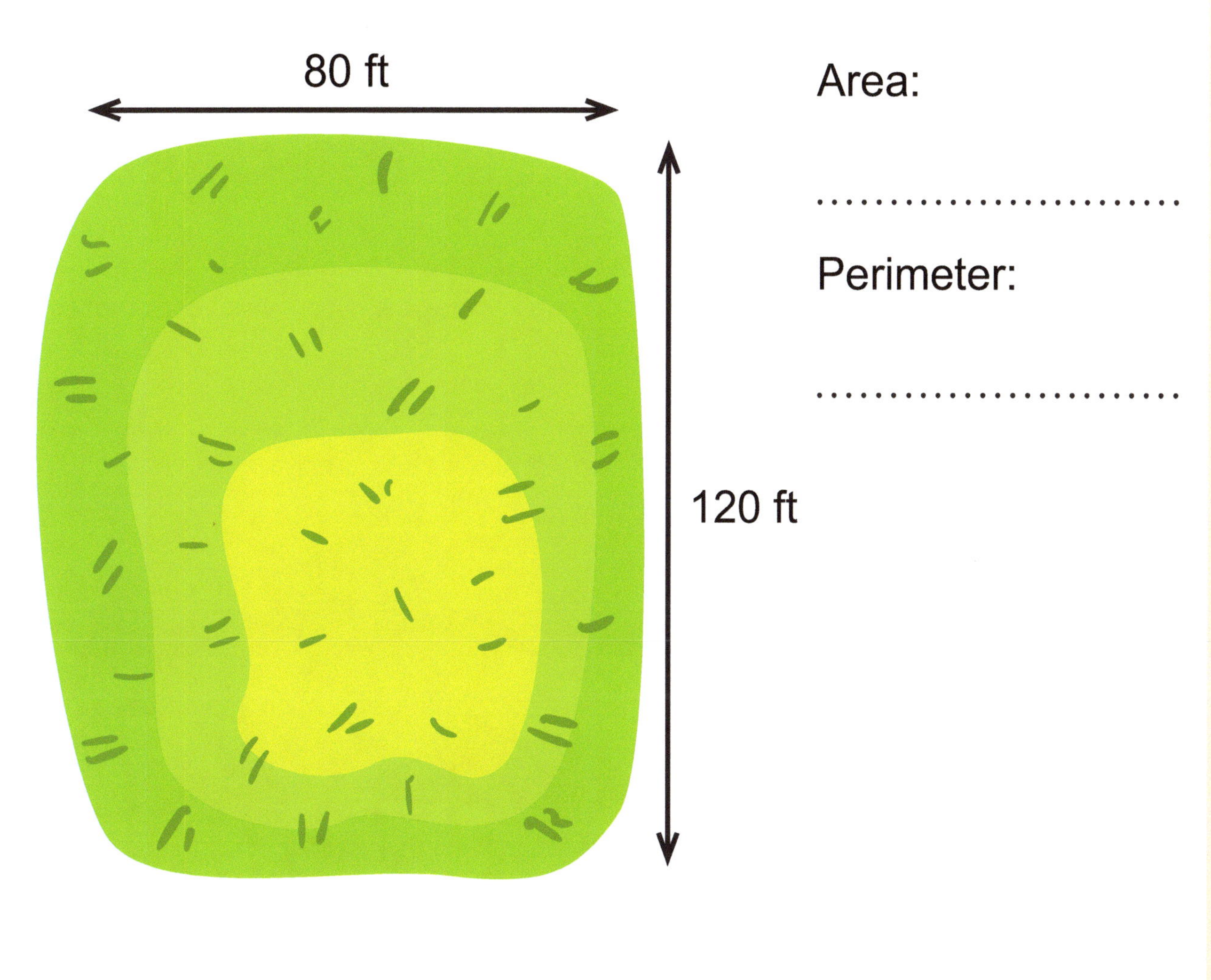

Mathematical Merry-Go-Round

How good are your rounding skills?

Name: _______________________   Class/Section: _______________________

Date: _______________________   Score: _______________________

Directions: Let's ride the merry-go-round! Round up the numbers on the horses and round down the numbers on the carriages. You have ten minutes to finish this activity!

IN THE FISHBOWL

Add and subtract the fish in the fishbowl.

Directions: We can't put too many fish in the fishbowls or they might be too crowded. Solve the addition and subtraction problems below to find out how many fish you can put in each bowl. Then color the number of fish that corresponds to your answer.

1.)  _________ + _________ = _________

2.)  _________ - _________ = _________

3.)  _________ + _________ = _________

4.)  _________ - _________ = _________

MULTIPLY AND COLOR!

Name:

Class/Section:

Date:

Score:

Instructions:
In this garden, you'll find multiplication problems. Answer each one correctly and complete the drawing by coloring. Have fun!

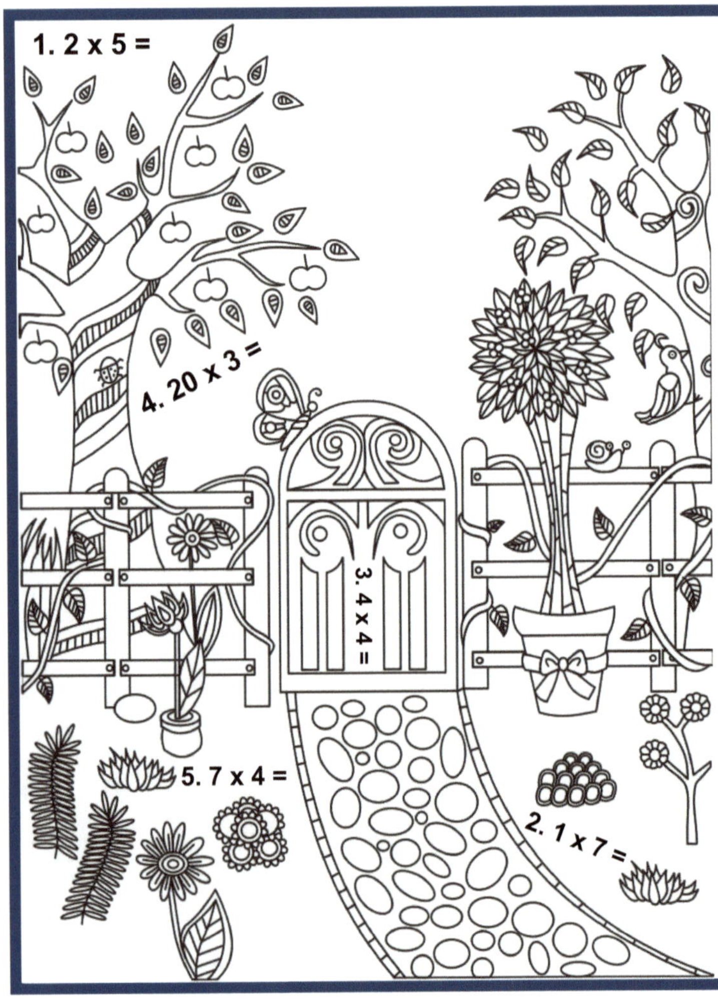

1. 2 x 5 =

4. 20 x 3 =

3. 4 x 4 =

5. 7 x 4 =

2. 1 x 7 =

Answers:

1. . . . .

2. . . . .

3. . . . .

4. . . . .

5. . . . .

SHAPE SORTER

Jai needs help sorting his things between flat shapes and solid forms. Can you help him out?
Circle the 2D shapes and box the 3D forms.

BUILD A CASTLE

CREATE A CASTLE USING DIFFERENT TRIANGLES!

NAME:

DATE:

SECTION:

SCORE:

Directions: Create the strong foundation for a castle by using different triangles. For every shape you draw, explain what kind of triangle it is (i.e. right, acute, obtuse, equilateral, isosceles, and scalene) then include its measurement.

Mathematics 201

· Conversion Method ·

Instructions: Study the blank metric ladder below. Write the correct order of units from the bottom going up. You are only given 5 minutes to complete the ladder. Kindly raise your hand once you're done.

mm | Kilometer | meter | centimeter

YOU CAN COUNT ON ME!

How many acorns can Mr. Squirrel collect?

Instructions: Count how many acorns there are and write the number
on this blank ______.

Sam Sells Seashells

Count how many seashells are sold by the seashore.

Directions: Add the numbers found in the two small seashells then jot down the answer on the big seashell. Be the first to submit your paper with all the correct answers to win a prize!

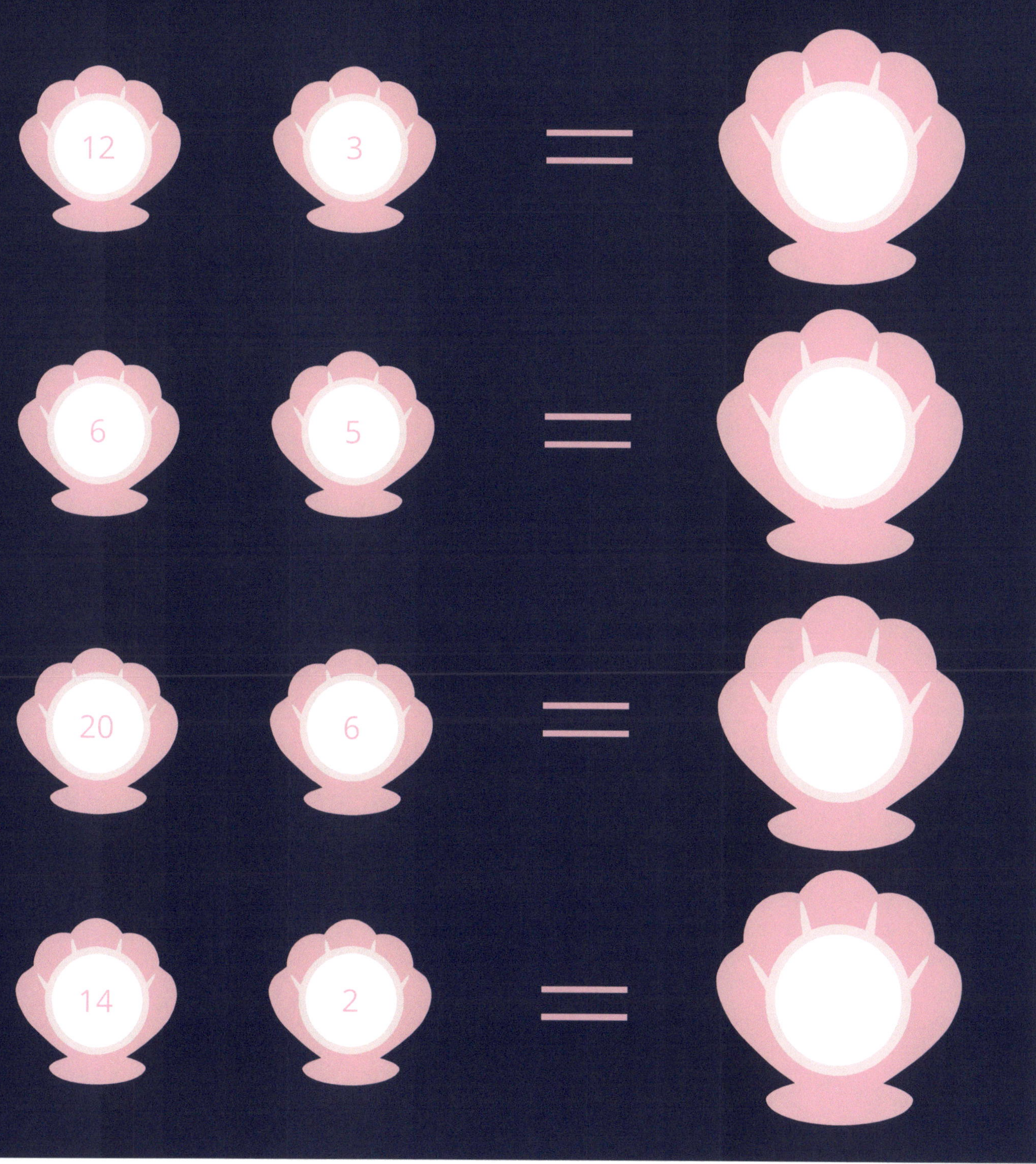

The Great Room Clean-up

Jeanie needs to clean up her room. Help her put her books in the book shelf and toys in the toy box.

You may not want to cut your workbook so copy the items at the bottom of the page onto a sheet of paper. Then cut along the dotted lines that you have drawn and then paste the pictures where they belong. How many books and toys does she have?

Book Shelf: _____ **books**

Toy Shelf: _____ **toys**

Prints and Patterns

Using the different materials you brought, create a unique pattern for each of the unicorns below. Combine geometric and organic shapes to make your patterns.

A MULTIPLICATION EXERCISE

TEST YOUR MULTIPLICATION SKILLS!

Directions: Multiply the numbers on the inner petals by the number on the center of the flower.
Place your answers on the outer petals.

Favorite Ice Cream Flavors

BAR GRAPH ACTIVITY SHEET

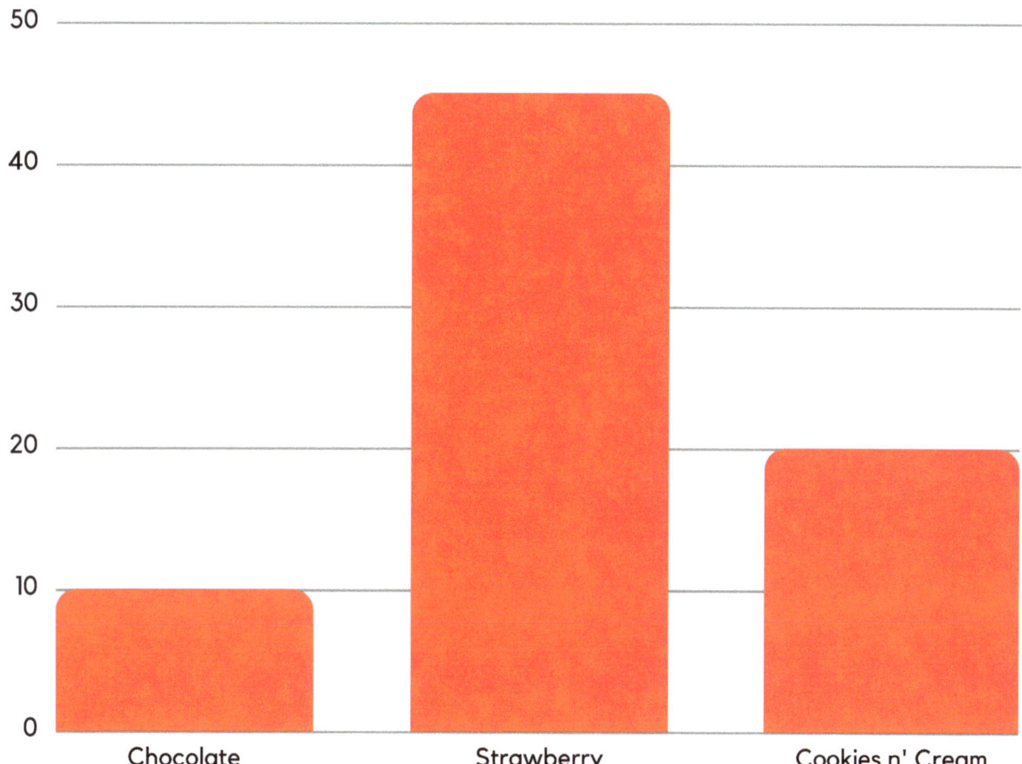

Use this bar graph to find out your classmates' favorite ice cream flavors.

1. Which ice cream flavor got the most votes?

2. Which ice cream flavor got the least votes?

3. How many more votes did "Chocolate" get than "Strawberry"?

4. How many more votes did "Cookies n' Cream" get than "Chocolate"?"

CANDY STORE

Jane is in a candy store and has three gold coins. She wants to get some strawberry bonbons! Three strawberry bonbons cost one gold coin. How much strawberry bonbons can Jane get with her three gold coins? Multiply and write your answer on the space below:

While at the candy store, Jane meets her friend Claire
who buys five mint candies. How many more candies
did Jane buy than Claire?

Claire's sister Lulu bought three toffee candies.
How many more candies did Claire buy than Lulu?

Who bought the least amount of candies?

BUILD A HOUSE!

Directions: Create a house by just using shapes such as circle, square, triangle and ractangle. You are given 30 minutes to complete the task. When done, you can color it in to make the shapes stand out. How many shapes is your house made of?

TIME TELLER'S TEST

DRAW HANDS ON THE CLOCK BASED ON THE TIME INDICATED BELOW.

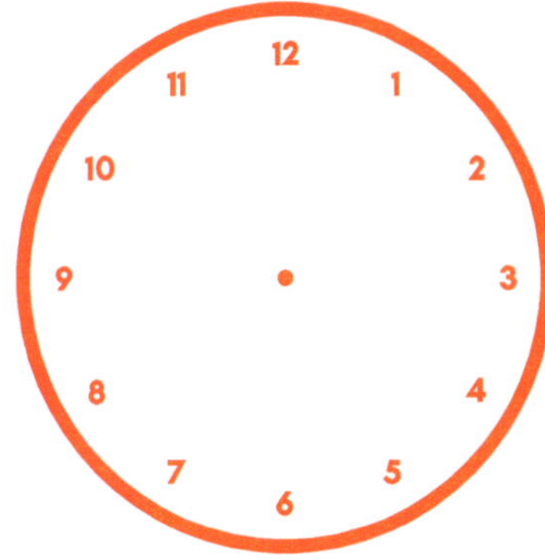

3:03 PM

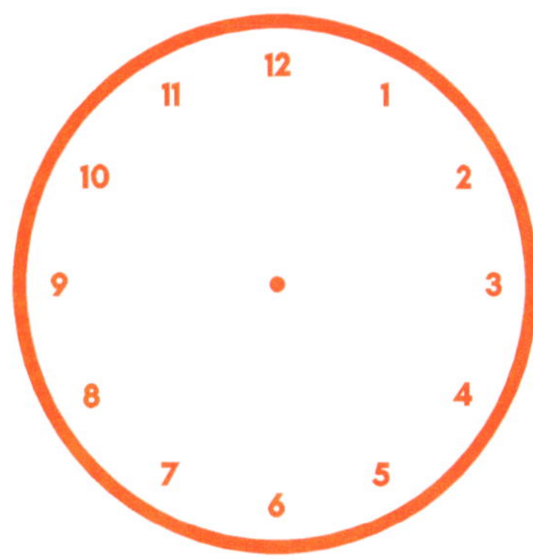

9:20 AM

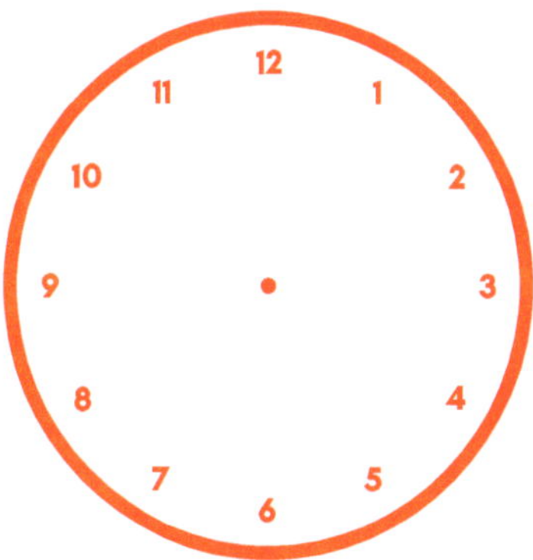

6:50 AM

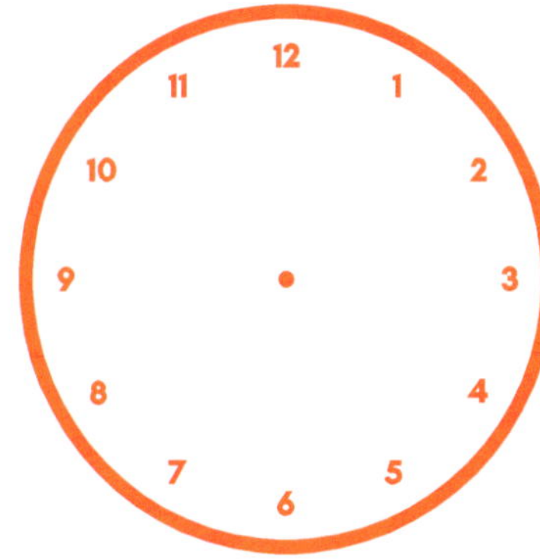

7:01 PM

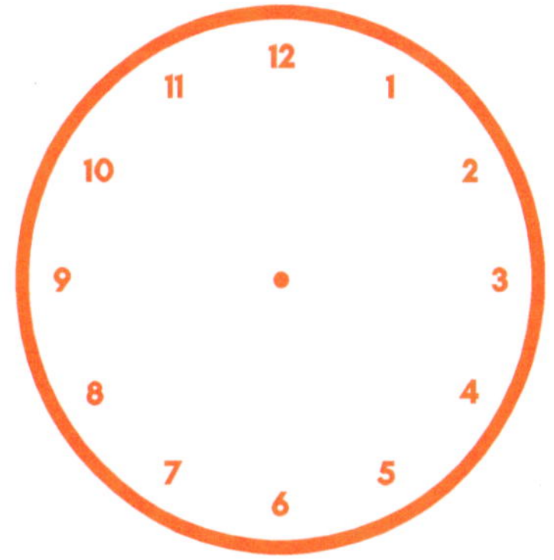

10:10 AM

Math Trick or Treating

WHICH SIDE HAS MORE?

Use >, <, and = to figure out which side has more treat bags, less treat bags, or the same number of treat bags

Let's draw a picture!

You have a wonderful smile! Using a mirror, draw your self portrait.

COLOR THAT SHAPE

Let's decorate this pizza! Follow the color guide and color the shapes. When done, count how many of each shape are in the pizza and write them in the boxes below.

Spot the Letters

Look at the letter on the left and circle the same letters on the row.

b	b	o	c	d	b	e
k	d	m	k	l	k	k
e	j	e	v	m	e	k
c	c	a	c	d	c	e
o	o	m	n	o	f	l
q	g	h	i	k	p	q
z	x	w	z	z	s	q

JOIN THE ROBOTS!

Pick up all of the robots from the game board. Start on the **B** circle. Do not pick up your pencil. Draw a line going left, right, up, or down. **Every line must end on a robot or the E circle. No stopping on an empty box.** Try to collect all the robots and end your last line on the E circle. You can go through a robot more than once.

Part of the line has already been drawn for you.

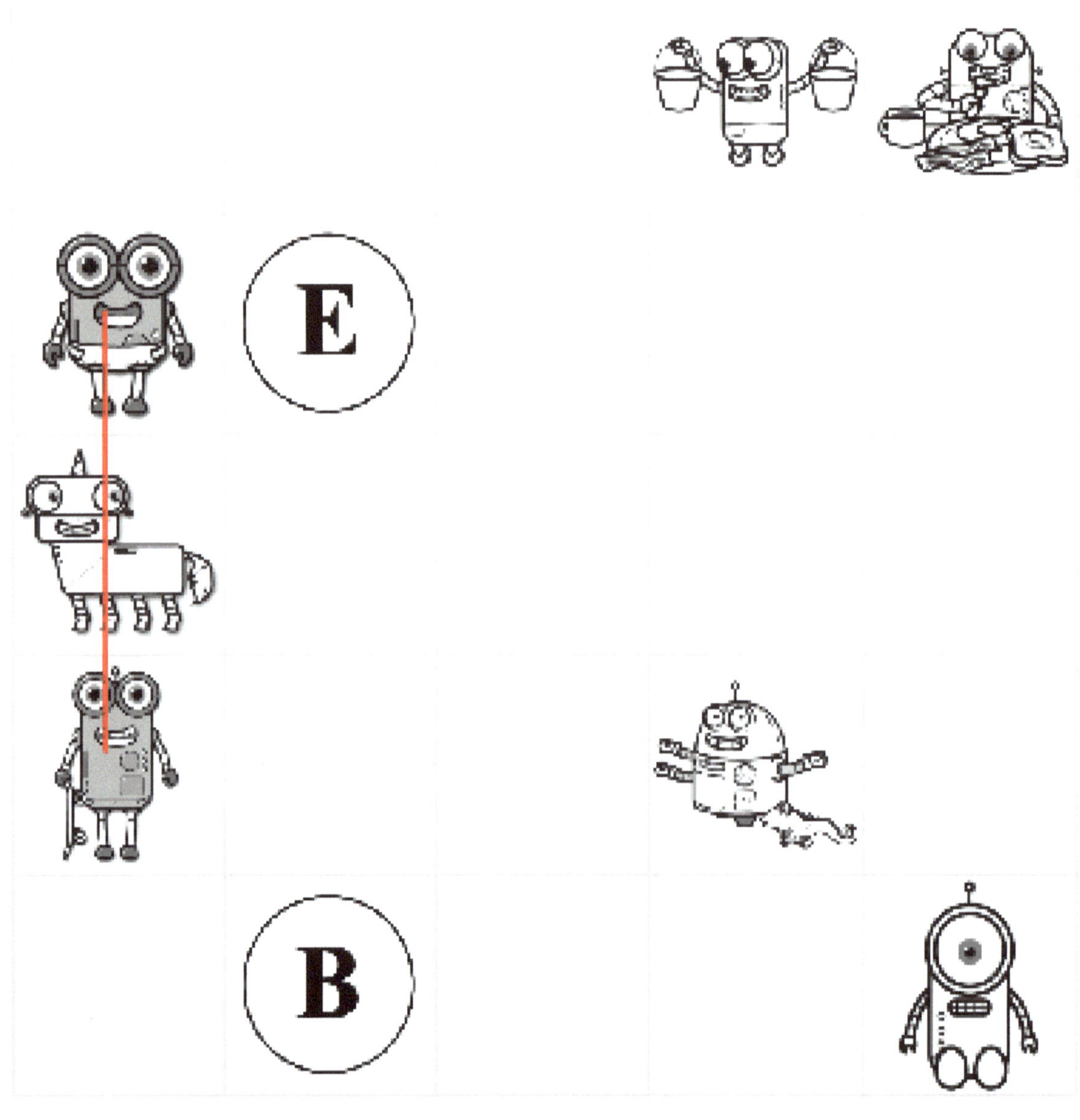

A Little Gardening Experiment

The gerbera flower is growing fast! Label the stages with numbers 1-7 to show the different growth stages of the plant from seedling to flower. What will help the plant grow quicker and taller?

If we grow one flower in a dim room inside the house and one out in the sunny garden, which one will grow faster? Why?